May I Have Your Attention, Please?

Your Guide to Business Writing That Charms, Captivates and Converts

Mish Slade

Copyright © Mish Slade 2016

All rights reserved. This book is sold subject to the condition that it shall not, by way of trade or otherwise, be lent, re-sold, hired out or otherwise circulated in any form of binding or cover other than that in which it is published and without a similar condition including this condition being imposed on the subsequent purchaser.

CONTENTS

Introduction	1
1: Show what you stand for	5
2: Niche it down	15
3: Be a human	23
4: Find your personality	41
5: Keep it simple	57
6: Sell the sizzle	61
7: Grab their attention	67
8: Follow your own path	81
9: Show, don't tell	85
10: Stay lean	93
11: Crush bad grammar	97
12: Blast through writer's block	109
Conclusion	117
Thank yous	119
About the author	121

BUSINESS WRITING BOOTCAMP – JOIN FOR FREE!

Sign up here: yourattentionplease.co/bootcamp

Business Writing Bootcamp is a six-part email series that helps you put everything in this book into action. It contains activities, exercises and tips galore – and it'll help you write captivating, enticing and profit-generating text in double-quick time!

What you'll get:

- Six detailed, example-filled emails from me over the course of a few weeks.

- Five downloadable activity sheets and templates, to help you practice (each one containing heaps of advice and ideas).

- Deconstructions of excellent business writing to see what works.

- Quick tips, tricks and hacks that I use when

writing for businesses.

- Personal help from me along the way.

Sign up for my FREE Business Writing Bootcamp here: yourattentionplease.co/bootcamp

INTRODUCTION

Something strange happens when people put finger to keyboard: they panic, give their personality the night off, then start to use words they'd *never* use in real life. By the time they've finished typing, it often looks like their sentences have been computed by a faulty robot.

This isn't too much of a big deal when it's just your dad emailing from vacation ("The weather is nice and we are having a nice time and I like utilizing the sun loungers. It is now dinner"), because you know your dad, and you can imagine what he'd actually be saying if you were face to face. But what about when it's *not* your dad's emails you're trying to reinterpret or reimagine – what about when it's the website text or brochure of a company you're thinking of using?

Or… scary-thought alert: what if it's YOUR web-

site or brochure text that lacks personality, imagination, or any semblance of humanness?

Your readers won't (I hope) all be friends and family who know how great you are and how valuable your service is. Your readers will be your prospective customers – people who don't know you and have no reason to stay on your page unless you make it compelling, entertaining and useful.

Most businesses get this horrendously wrong because they don't consider what readers want to get out of the experience. Instead, they focus on trying to sound professional, experienced or knowledgeable – and it almost always backfires. They "leverage" this, "synergize" that, and offer "integrated, innovative solutions" for just about everything else. They use words that no one ever says out loud, come across as stiff and wooden in the process, and have a remarkable knack for saying nothing of interest about anything – least of all what they can do for their customers.

And that's a shame, because those businesses often have fantastic stuff to sell.

Why do they get it so wrong? There are many reasons (and I touch on them throughout this book), but the most damaging of all is that they forget they're selling to *people.* Whether those people are individual consumers or buying on behalf of their company, it doesn't matter: their emotions and feelings will *always* play a part in their decision making. **Your job as a business owner is to make the buying decision easy for them.**

It's about communicating what you do, what you stand for, and why you're the *only* choice for them. It won't be easy, but it'll be worth it: your text can become your very best salesperson, working 24/7 to convince readers to become your next customers.

Once you've crafted the sort of copy that makes people reflexively reach for their credit cards, everything becomes easier. For one thing, you get to charge higher prices. A big reason so many businesses compete on price is because they can't prove what value they offer, so they're stuck with the one selling point that's a *breeze* to communicate: cheapness. If you pride yourself on the quality of your service or product, it's no damn fun to run a business where people only buy from you because you're less expensive than your competitors.

This book will give you the means to charge those higher prices. You'll learn how to write in a way that's lively and full of personality. How to cut the crap and stand out from the competition. How to make your readers recognize your brilliance and trust you implicitly. And how to have an unlikely amount of fun with words.

Ready to get started? All you need is an understanding of what your business is about, a willingness to do things a bit differently, and a teensy bit of patience (to help get you through a couple of my frustrated outbursts... I promise they don't last long). You **don't** need to be a writer, and I don't expect you to have any detailed knowledge of English grammar.

Here goes!

Mish (mish@mortifiedcow.com)

p.s. Sign up to my **FREE Business Writing Bootcamp**, and put everything from this book into practice: **yourattentionplease.co/bootcamp**

Chapter 1
SHOW WHAT YOU STAND FOR

"People don't buy what you do; they buy why you do it." –Simon Sinek

The reason I own a Mac isn't because I think it's better than a PC (although it is, but that's a debate for another day). My preference for Warby Parker glasses isn't because they're higher quality than other brands – and they're *definitely* not the cheapest. My Tom Bihn backpack is one of the best-designed, most durable items I've ever bought – but it cost a fortune and I'm sure there are plenty of less expensive alternatives that are just as good.

I didn't just choose those products because I think

they're great – I chose them (even if only on a subconscious level) because of what I think they say about me and how I want to be perceived by others. I chose them because each of those brands stands for more than just the product they create.

We all do it, and not just for personal items: in all areas of life, we like to buy and use products and services that extend our self-identity. In choosing one company over another, we're choosing to say something about ourselves and what we stand for... and that's because *we're buying into what the company says about **itself** and what **it** stands for.*

If you want to appeal to potential customers, your product or service has to be excellent, of course. But it needs a lot more than that: it needs to stand for something that your potential customers can get behind and believe in.

Your company *will* stand for something, even if you don't know what it is yet. Think back to why you started it in the first place, and look through customer emails and testimonials to discover what they love about you.

If you make cupcakes, do you believe that cupcakes ought to be eaten by adults, at night, with a glass of wine? If you're an accountant for small businesses, are you struck by how other accountants make things seem far more complicated than they need to? If you're a dentist, do you think that strong, healthy teeth are more important than straight, white ones? If you're a New York-based wedding photographer, do you believe that NYC deserves to be the "bridesmaid" of every shot? If you're a technology company, do you believe that "the crazy ones" and "the misfits" are the ones who'll change the world with the help of your products? If you're a website designer, do you think it's your job to be stubborn and insistent with your clients for their own good? (Those last three have already been taken – see the examples on the following pages.)

Whatever you do, make sure it's something unique to your business – something that couldn't be said for all the other players in your industry. This is where many businesses go wrong. They say vague things like:

- *"Focused on building rewarding relationships."*

- *"Dedicated to YOUR success."*
- *"Going the extra mile for you."*
- *"Consistently delivering successful projects."*

These claims mean nothing, they could be said by anyone, and no one feels *anything* after reading them.

Once you've pinpointed what you stand for, bear in mind that you might not even need to announce what it is on your site – it might be implicit in how you write and what you choose to say. Once you've identified it though, you'll find that everything you write is much easier as a result.

Want some inspiration? Take a look at the next few pages.

THESE COMPANIES SHOW WHAT THEY STAND FOR...

WORKHORSE PRINT MAKERS

Nothing says love like heavy metal.

We don't mean purple satin, long hair and guitars heavy metal. We mean one ton of cast iron slowly squeezing paper in its tender embrace. We mean men lavishing attention on long forgotten machines that once were the epoch of human ingenuity. Hammers hitting steel, the squeak of belts, and the sizzle of oil on well lubed bushings. We love letterpress.

People used to make things with blood and toil and sleepless nights. Nothing you truly care about can be made by a nameless face in a far flung country and left out in the rain on your porch the next day. Our investment to you is missed parties, skinned knuckles, and an alarm that comes too early. We do it because we care about the things we make. More importantly we do it because we care about the things we make for you.

Workhorse Printmakers is a full service letterpress print shop proud to call Houston, Texas home. We use environmentally friendly soy based inks and citrus solvents. Our house stocks are recycled or tree free cotton and American made if possible. We're not perfect but we try.

(workhorseprints.com)

MULE DESIGN

Stubborn. *When you've got a stubborn design problem, you need a stubborn designer. (We don't mean a jerk. No one needs that.) We're talking about someone who really commits — to understanding what you need and to getting it right.*

We're stubborn because we love design. We love how design can help people. Good choices make work effortless, make meaning clear, and make the otherwise mundane, enthralling. Good design can also make money. And we like money. Maybe you do, too.

(muledesign.com)

B-FREED WEDDINGS (PHOTOGRAPHY)

I believe that at the core of humanity there's jazz.

I believe you should drive with the heat on and sunroof open during the dead of winter.

I believe you should cuddle with your dog at least once a day.

I was born and raised in New York, and it is my goal to make New York City a bridesmaid at your wedding! I love to incorporate all of what this spectacular city has to offer in the photos I make for you, from the one-of-a-kind Central Park, to the cobblestone streets of SoHo, to the skyscrapers in Mid-Town. I'm not just a tour guide and photographer – I'm here to help plan and document your NYC adventure! You've arrived and put yourself in the city; I'm going to put the city into you!

(b-freedweddings.com/brian)

APPLE

Here's to the crazy ones. The misfits. The rebels. The troublemakers. The round pegs in the square holes.

The ones who see things differently. They're not fond of rules. And they have no respect for the status quo. You can quote them, disagree with them, glorify or vilify them.

About the only thing you can't do is ignore them. Because they change things. They invent. They imagine. They heal. They explore. They create. They inspire. They push the human race forward.

Maybe they have to be crazy.

How else can you stare at an empty canvas and see a work of art? Or sit in silence and hear a song that's never been written? Or gaze at a red planet and see a laboratory on wheels?

We make tools for these kinds of people.

While some see them as the crazy ones, we see genius. Because the people who are crazy enough to think they can change the world, are the ones who do.

(apple.com)

Chapter 2
NICHE IT DOWN

"You have to understand that nothing appeals to everybody." –Gene Simmons

Just for a moment, imagine that you have curly, difficult-to-manage hair. It's been driving you crazy for years, but you've come to realize that it's never going to be your best feature. You'll never be the one with the "great hair" – and these days you're happy being the one with the "fabulous ankles" instead.

Then your usual hair salon closes down, and you're in need of a new place to get your hair cut. You jump on a few message boards and learn about a new salon nearby that specializes in curly hair. Whaaat? "That exists?" you think to yourself.

"That's incredible!"

Well, such a salon actually *does* exist. It's called Ouidad (ouidad.com), and its flagship store is in NYC. The salon's mission statement is about "empowering individuals with curly hair to understand, enhance and love their hair," and the website has heaps of guidance about "understanding your curl" and "identifying your curl." There's also information about their special trademarked cutting technique for curls, and a range of *"How much???"*-priced products.

The cost of a haircut is almost double what you're used to paying, but… well, it's a no-brainer, isn't it? You're going to make an appointment without hesitating. Your search ends here: no more Googling or message board trawling for you. What's more, you're *ridiculously* excited about your upcoming salon session, you can't wait to speak to your stylist about your hair woes, and you already know you'll buy up half their products while you're there. When it comes to paying for your fabulous new haircut, there won't be a sharp intake of breath: you'll be too excited by the experience you've just had.

This is the benefit of niching down, and not enough businesses make the most of it. In fact, too many businesses try to do the precise opposite: they try to appeal to everyone, and they end up resonating with no one.

By focusing on a tight niche, everything becomes more straightforward: you can speak directly to a particular audience and address their specific needs (which means you can also dispense with all that infuriatingly vague stuff about "Whether you're a large, small or medium-sized business..."). You don't need to compete on price, because you'll be the obvious choice for those people. Marketing becomes simpler, because there's less guesswork about where your dream customer will find you. And you'll become so knowledgeable about your niche that these people will trust you and refer you more and more.

If you don't niche down, you risk ending up writing baloney like this:

"My goal is to help small, medium or large business

owners, such as yourself, spend less time working in your business and more time working on your business. In the end, you'll be spending less total time working and will be making more money. I'd also like to help you put the FUN back in your business and your life. My goal is to help you BUILD a strong team, GROW the business, Get RESULTS, Be PROFITable and reach your DREAMS." (Business consultant)

This text tries to cover all bases with the target customer, while taking a few random guesses at their desired outcome. Focusing on a tighter market wouldn't have solved every single problem with the wording, but it would certainly have helped.

Niching down doesn't *have* to be about focusing on a subset of your market or even a particular service within your industry – so you won't need to completely restructure your business if it's already up and running. You can achieve a similar outcome by having a strong, confident personality that makes your dream customers feel ecstatic to have found you.

Take Print Hut (printhut.co.uk), for example – a UK company that provides standard printing services. Rather than try to appeal to a subset of a large market (people who need printing services), they've decided to niche down by appealing to a particular *type* of person: someone who likes their services to be a bit zany. The bright colors of the site combined with fun, humorous writing may not interest your average CEO of a Fortune 500, but it'll be loved by the target audience.

Here are some more examples of businesses niching down:

- No Fear Dentists (nofeardentists.com) is "dedicated to anxious patients." If you're scared of the dentist, you're going to go here rather than any other surgery around, right? Take a look at the site, and you'll see that everything's been written with anxious patients in mind.

- Are you an entrepreneur in need of a shrink? Who are you more likely to choose – a generic psychiatrist who'll treat anyone, or Peter Shallard, the "Shrink for Entrepreneurs" (petershallard.com)? Peter's blog has become well-known among internet entrepreneurs in particular, and it's a marketing tool in itself: people see that he really knows what he's talking about, and – if they need a shrink – they'll get in touch without hesitation.

- JoeArchitect (joearchitect.com) is an architectural and interior design firm specializing in dental office design in North America. If you're setting up your own dental office in North America, *surely* you'd choose them over any old architect? Once you've read their site and seen just how much they know about your industry, you'll find it hard to hire anyone else.

- If you own a vegan business and need marketing expertise, you'll be wanting Vegan Mainstream – a company that specializes in marketing for vegan bloggers, authors, business owners and entrepreneurs (veganmainstream.com). They're bound to catch your attention over and above all the other marketing services available.

- Medical Marketing Solutions (medmarketing.co) does exactly what you'd imagine: marketing for companies in the medical industry (physical therapy centers, spine centers, healthcare product providers, dental surgeries, etc.). It means they get to say this kind of thing on their website, and truly appeal to their target customer: "From HIPPA violations and Stark law, to the Anti-Kickback Statute and the Sunshine Act, Medical Marketing Solutions has a team well-versed not only in successful marketing strategies, but successful marketing strategies that abide by the laws and guidelines specific to the medical community."

If you can't immediately think of a way to niche down your business, you'll find some useful guidance in this blog post: bit.ly/inc-niche.

Chapter 3
BE A HUMAN

"If you're not a person who says 'indeed' or 'moreover,' or who calls someone an individual… please don't write it." –William Zinsser

I bet you don't know anyone who *actually* talks like this:

> *"We have revolutionized excellence through success and ideation. We provide unrivalled strategic partnerships together with a plethora of live, social and communication solutions. Our client-centric approach delivers seamlessly integrated relations ensuring a unique and amplified user experience." (An events company… I think)*

What on earth does any of that mean?!

Or how about this:

> "Individuals and businesses that seek professional accounting services can choose from a long list of firms with a variety of attributes. With that in mind, we believe every client that chooses to enlist our firm to navigate the tax code on its behalf pays us a great compliment that warrants our dedication to provide the very best service available. We're grateful for the confidence our clients place in us, and we're committed to delivering results that earn their continued confidence for years to come." (Accountancy firm)

These examples are taken from websites run by humans – not robots, surprisingly.

If I look past the lack of niching down, the ZERO personality, the lackluster intros and the complete inability to sell the sizzle (which I talk about more later), my *other* beef with these pieces of text is that they're not how a person would speak in real life.

Is this a bad thing? Yes – if you want people to read and understand what you write. Yes – if you want to build rapport with them on the page. And yes –

if you want to make your offer to them clear. When businesses don't know what they're offering, they resort to clichés and/or formal, robotic language. When they use engaging, straightforward language, however, it shows they have both a clear vision and the competence to achieve it.

Taking the second paragraph as an example (because I seriously have no clue what the first one is about), how would people express those sentiments out loud? They might say something like:

> *"You've got a lot of choice when it comes to picking an accountant: there are hundreds of us in your zip code alone! And yet we know we can do a better job than the others – and that you'll be delighted by both our service and the financial results we can achieve for you."*

To be clear, this second attempt is nowhere near good enough for a business site – and you'll see why as you read the rest of this book. Yet it's still miles better than the original version, because it's easy to read and it feels more human.

Here's some writing guidance to help you come

across as the human(s) you hopefully are:

1: There's nothing wrong with contractions.

We use contractions (won't, we'll, I'll, I'd, you'd, they're…) all the time when we talk – and we should use them when we write, too. Otherwise everything just reads like an academic thesis.

So…

- "Here is some guidance." –> "Here's some guidance."

- "You will not regret hiring us." –> "You won't regret hiring us."

- "It is going to be an exciting day for all involved." –> "It's going to be an exciting day for all involved."

2: The best way to address your reader? "You."

Not "the client" or (god forbid) "the stakeholder." This goes for all written material – brochures, website text, social media posts, etc.

The reader should feel like they're being talked to

directly, as part of a one-on-one conversation.

3: You, meanwhile, are "we" (or "I").

There are times when you'll have no choice but to use the name of your business or "the company" in place of "I" or "we," but they're rare. Try substituting "I" or "we" for the company name wherever possible; it almost always works better and comes across as more personable.

Here's an example to show how effective it is at humanizing a company:

Original text:

> *"The members of the Newark law firm of Robinson Miller LLC have been litigating business matters successfully for their clients for decades. The firm's experienced attorneys understand and appreciate their clients' need to resolve business disputes strategically and cost-effectively. Their sensitivity to the clients' business interests, together with their in-depth knowledge of substantive law and the intricacies of practice in the Federal and State courts of New Jersey, achieve their clients'*

goals." (Litigation lawyers)

New text:

"We've been litigating business matters successfully for our clients for decades. Our experienced attorneys understand and appreciate your needs to resolve business disputes strategically and cost-effectively. Our sensitivity to your business interests, together with our in-depth knowledge of substantive law and the intricacies of practice in the Federal and State courts of New Jersey, achieve your goals."

The new text still needs an awful lot of work, but simply changing "the firm" and "the client" to "we" and "you" makes the text feel *far* less corporate-drone-y and tons more friendly.

4: Business clichés and vagueness are for people who don't know what they're trying to say.

If you "help businesses build better solutions," or you "help businesses succeed," or you "offer integrated solutions," or you "craft experiences," or you "engage with businesses and consumers," or you "drive innovation," or you "advocate an entrepreneurial environment," or you "deliver measurable results," or you "create organizational efficiencies," or you "solve business challenges," or you "help businesses concentrate on what they do best," or you offer a "bespoke" or "tailored" service, or you "focus on customer engagement," or you "create immersive experiences," or you "use cross-channel tactics"… please stop. No one has a clue what you *actually* do – and there's a chance you don't either.

These words should be used, well, never. But they are – frequently – and sometimes all at once, in the case of this financial advice company:

"Tailored solutions

BESPOKE FINANCIAL PLANNING

Freeing up your time for what you do best"

It all goes back to showing what you stand for (Chapter 1). Once you've figured out what you want to achieve for your client, you no longer have to rely on vague, nothing-y phrases – and you can win your readers over with concrete, exciting text that describes exactly what they're looking for.

5: "Fancy" words are anything but.

- "Utilize" is lame and pretentious. You mean "use."

- "Amongst" and "whilst" (used to an annoying degree among British businesses) can most probably be replaced with "among" and "while."

- "Yourself" and "myself" are almost always used incorrectly. Stick with "you" and "me."

- "Ensure" something if you must, but you can probably "make sure" of it instead.

- Do you wish to "facilitate," or just "help"?

- Much of the time, "regarding" can be swapped out for "about." ("For more information ~~regarding~~ about this project, email me.")

- If you want to talk about "the present time,"

you could just say "now."

- You can "show" rather than "indicate," "finish" rather than "finalize," "place" or "put" rather than "position," and "start" instead of "initiate."

6: Get to the point.

In business writing, people love to do a lot of "corporate throat-clearing": couching their words in long-winded preambles in which they announce that they're in the act of saying something:

"We are writing to express our regrets that we are unable to attend your launch party next week."

Rather than: "We're sorry, but we can't make your launch party."

Or: "I wish to congratulate you on your new job."

Rather than: "Congratulations!"

The shorter version is always more natural and conversational – not to mention warmer and more sincere.

7: Bury dead verbs and nouns.

You don't deliver change to your car; you just change your car. You don't deliver cooking to your family; you simply cook for your family. (You also don't "deliver on" or "deliver against" anything.)

You don't drive improvements in your fitness; you improve your fitness.

So why do you "deliver change" to your business, or "drive improvements" in your processes? If you get rid of all these dead words, you'll instantly sound more like a human being.

8: Keep paragraphs flowing.

There are far too many overlong sentences in the world, which require the reader to wade through them while keeping track of everything that's being said.

Like this:

> *"Known as Canada's mid-market alternative for audit, tax and advisory solutions, we have developed a reputation for being a real choice for quality*

and value added financial advice due to the depth and breadth of in-house skills, customized offerings, commitment to excellence in customer service and our global reach." (Accountancy firm)

Aaaand breathe.

On the other hand, you don't want a series of short, jumpy sentences either: it's unnatural. It's not how we speak.

Ideally you want a natural-sounding mixture: a few mid-length sentences, a couple of long ones that contain useful information expertly explained, and a few short fragments to keep readers alert.

If you have trouble writing anything shorter than spaghetti-like, gasp-for-breath sentences, there's a good chance you can delete a ton of words without losing your original meaning. If that's not the case, try identifying the main points you want to make, and turn each point into a separate sentence.

Read your work out loud before you hit "publish." Does it sound like regular, natural conversation? That's what you want to aim for: not only will your reader get the sense that you're a real, live person (or group of people), but they'll also find it easier to glide through your words and understand everything you have to say.

Don't forget about punctuation, by the way! You can usually tell if a sentence has been punctuated correctly by reading it out loud.

Here's a billboard ad for you to practice on:

> *"Without perfect black you cannot have perfect colour and perfect black can only be produced by the self-emitting pixels within LG OLED technology." (Electronics company)*

The first half of this sentence is a MESS: it's so badly punctuated I can't believe it actually made it onto a poster. The effect? Aside from looking unprofessional and shoddy, it isn't all that easy to read or make sense of. (There's also no warmth, no humanness: it feels like it's been written like a machine.)

It needs to say something like this instead:

> *"Without perfect black, you can't achieve perfect colour. And there's only one way to achieve perfect*

black: through the self-emitting pixels used in our LG OLED technology."

With the help of correct punctuation, this second version has a better pace and more natural flow.

9: No one will kill you if you use "and" at the start of a sentence.

The same goes for "but" and "because." They'll make your sentences come across as friendlier and more natural (after all, we do it the whole time when we speak).

10: Get active.

Active sentences are sentences where the subject is doing the action. They're shorter, more dynamic, and less wimpy than passive sentences (where something is being "done" to the object of the sentence).

Here are some examples:

- "We'll ship the merchandise tomorrow." (Active)

- "The merchandise will be shipped

tomorrow." (Passive)

- "You can find more information on our website." (Active)

- "More information can be found on our website." (Passive)

Politicians often use the passive voice to avoid taking responsibility: "Mistakes were made."

In most cases, active = better. You can use the passive form (or "The passive form can be used...") if you don't know who's doing the action, or if you think that the object receiving the action is more important or should be emphasized: "The project will be finished by 5pm sharp."

I found the following abomination of a passive paragraph on the website of a lighting design practice:

> *"A dominant feature to the fifth floor was the introduction of a cantilevered wine cellar which projects from the side of the building. To ensure this still felt as if it was 'floating' the onyx floor was backlit. The exceptional wine collection is discretely lit with tiny*

inset LEDs whilst the central pendant warms the brickwork and assists in balancing the layers of light. The beautiful tiled kitchen ceiling is framed by linear lighting set within the original steel beams."

The whole thing could sound SO much more human, friendly and energetic if parts of it had been written in the active voice:

"A dominant feature of the fifth floor is a spectacular cantilevered wine cellar, which projects from the side of the building. We applied backlights to the cellar's onyx floor to make it feel like it's "floating," and we used a central light pendant to warm the brickwork and balance the layers of light. The beautiful tiled kitchen ceiling is framed by linear lighting set within the original steel beams, and we made sure to show off the main attraction – the exceptional wine collection – with tiny, discretely lit, inset LEDs."

To sum up... this guidance is useful for when you're about to write something from scratch, but it's also handy for helping you fix existing text: it will help you understand *why* your writing doesn't feel very human or natural.

For example, you might have once written something like this and been unable to pinpoint why it doesn't feel quite right:

> *"This is because the Bolds Creative team is not limited within the rigid boundaries of traditionally defined roles. Instead, they come together as a group of talented multidisciplinary experts poised to meet a diverse set of challenges." (Design agency)*

Some reasons might be:

- The lack of contractions sounds robotic and unnatural ("this is"; "is not").

- They refer to themselves in the third person ("Bolds Creative"; "they come together"). When speaking on the phone – even to clients – they'd almost never do this. Instead they'd use "we".

- Who would ever say "multidisciplinary experts poised to meet a diverse set of challenges" out loud? It makes hard work of a very simple message.

Assuming the company wants to keep to a fairly serious tone, they could easily transform the above paragraph into something that's a little livelier and more natural to read – like this:

> *"Everyone on the team has multiple talents and a wide range of skills, so we've done away with the old-school company structure and traditional job titles. Instead, we blend all our abilities together into a magical, non-conformist mixture that creates truly extraordinary marketing ideas for your business."*

HOW TO BE A HUMAN

Try these exercises to help you write in a more human way:

- Rather than write anything down, record yourself speaking what you want to say – and imagine you're telling your friend/mom/partner rather than your potential customer. Transcribe what you say, and work from there. You should find that there are fewer clichés, less jargon, and that the sentences flow together far more naturally.

- Talk to a person who *could* be a dream customer of yours, and tell them about your business. Whenever they get confused, use different words and phrases until they understand and get excited about whatever you're offering. Write down those words and phrases!

- Address the piece of text to a friend or relative (literally write "Dear [name]" at the top). You'll need to do a fair bit of editing once you've written the piece, but you'll be working from something that's far more human in tone – and that's the hardest thing to get right.

- Also bear in mind that you'll need to insert more personality into your words than when you're talking in real life: you won't have the smiling eyes, or over-the-top gesticulations, or the cadence of an actual, audible voice to rely on.

Chapter 4
FIND YOUR PERSONALITY

"To me, business isn't about wearing suits or pleasing stockholders. It's about being true to yourself, your ideas, and focusing on the essentials." –Richard Branson

If your company were a person, what sort of person would it be? Witty? Sarcastic? Silly? No-nonsense? Spiritual? Classy? A snob?

Don't know? **You need to find out.**

"Personality" is why I sometimes wish I had facial hair – just so I could get a monthly razor subscription from Dollar Shave Club (dollarshaveclub.com). And it's why my husband is desperate to visit Adventure Bar in London (adventurebar.co.uk/about-us) – even though he doesn't drink, hates bars, and prefers to spend his evenings reading about mortgage interest rates. The respective personalities of these two brands appeal to us; they draw us in and make us want to buy from them. (I've included text from these brands – as well as many other brands mentioned in this chapter – on the following pages.)

When your business has a personality, it gives people the opportunity to think "YES!!! THIS IS BRILLIANT" or "good god, no" within seconds – and that's a good thing. If they're reading your website and it's a bit "meh," they might decide to keep the tab open... but then the computer will do one of those unwarranted automatic updates, the tab will disappear and the reader will never, ever return.

As I said in Chapter 2, a brand personality can also be seen as an extension of "niching down" your business. In fact, it's what my husband and I do with our copywriting business, Mortified Cow (mortifiedcow.com). To a lot of people, our name is saying "We're not serious enough for your Very

Important Business. Go over there and talk to Platinum Corporate Solutions instead." Which is exactly the idea, because we don't want to work with anyone who thinks business has to be buttoned-up and stuffy.

Remember: buying decisions almost always involve an element of emotion – and your job is to make your dream customers *feel* like you're the right fit for them. The "YES!!!" people are the ones who'll immediately be sold on the idea of working with you – and they'll be willing to pay a premium to do so, too.

Many years ago I wrote the "about" page copy for my dad's jewelry website (smoochrings.co.uk/about-us), and his customers still mention it as the reason why they went with him over his competitors: they love how jovial, self-deprecating and enthusiastic about his work he is. There are bound to be lots of people who want something more polished and professional-sounding from a man who's about to sell them thousands of pounds worth of jewelry, but that's fine: they can go elsewhere. My dad, meanwhile, will be left with his dream customers – the ones who already like him, appreciate his humorous take on everything, and understand how he can help them.

TOMS shoes (toms.com) is another example of a company that has – perhaps unintentionally – cultivated a "love or loathe" personality for itself. Many people can't bear what they perceive to be its smug, self-congratulatory attitude – and yet there are plenty of loyal, loving supporters who'll buy up every new product on offer. Dividing opinion is a good thing: you won't get this sort of devotion if you're bland and run-of-the-mill.

Having a strong brand personality is about more than just an assertive "about" page or mission statement: it's often the smallest touches that give the biggest glimpses into a company's personality. Just take a look at Tumblr (tumblr.com) – the almost-*too*-easy-to-use microblogging service with quirky, personalityful copy by the bucketload. Even its error messages have character: if you try to log in without typing your email address and password, it sarcastically informs you, "You do have to fill this stuff out, you know." Not everyone's going to love that, but it'll no doubt appeal to Tumblr's target audience.

Just like Tumblr, you need to weave your chosen personality through every aspect of your business, or else it doesn't work. If you have super-funny Twitter text but a dull, dead website, for example, you'll seem inauthentic and untrustworthy.

But WHAT sort of personality should you go for? Think about what sort of customer you want to have, and work back from there. If you're an accountancy firm and you want to attract serious-minded bankers who are short on time but big on worry, a fun 'n' breezy, joke-laden approach might not be the way to go. If, on the other hand, you want to attract small business owners who like a bit of banter, such an approach might be perfect. The Wow Company in the UK went down the latter route: their website's "What we do" page allows you to create your own package of services in the same style as ordering a pizza with all your favorite toppings: thewowcompany.com/what-we-do

It's possible that your own personality is perfect for the business, or you might decide to go with something a bit different. Either is fine – as long as it doesn't feel forced or unnatural, and you remember that the written personality must be consistent with how you and your staff come across when you start doing business. If you're quite a serious person, it might be safer to leave the written humor to others. For an example of non-jokey-yet-awesome text in action, take a look at the Blu Homes website (bluhomes.com/our-vision): they do a fantastic job of infusing passion, dedication and care into their words.

Whichever personality route you go down, just remember to choose something and commit to it. When your company has a personality, you automatically stand apart from everyone else in your industry. And let's not forget that it's way more fun to write something that has charm and individuality rather than the dreary, bleurgh nonsense you get from most businesses.

Check out the following examples for inspiration.

PERSONALITY BY THE BUCKETLOAD...

ADVENTURE BAR

Adventure Bar has one of the funnest "about" pages out there. The grammar is a tad wonky at times, but they're able to just about get away with it:

*EVERYONE LIKES
A LITTLE ADVENTURE!*

*...it's a bit like riding a **Burning Red Mustang Sally** through **Key West** with an **Umpa Lumpa** while **Ziggy Stardust** has **Sex On The Beach** with a **Porn Star**... or at least that's what some branding agency said. once.*

its important that you read this in a booming deity like voice...

Our dream has always been to deliver a great time via the medium of great food and great drinks, with service that makes you smile and tunes that make you wish you owned this record. On vinyl. We want to do it in settings that make you say WOW, but in a good way like when that austrian guy jumped from outer space and everyone went bananas for a week and no one slept 'cause they drank so much energy drink. Not WOW like you've just seen a slightly disturbing video involving gerbils on youtube.

We want people that love life. We want people that love drinking and eating with us. We want people that make us laugh. We want it all and most worryingly,

We.

Want.

You.

The dream started a long time ago, back when all of this was black and white and people used to listen to the shipping forecast for fun, nowadays together, we bring the fun.

To make all of this happen, we employ people with big personalities, scandinavians with funny accents and french people with crazy beards, not because they are cool in a 'pointy shoes riding a fixie kind of way', but in a cool 'I wish he was my friend' kind of way. Then we train them in a gruelling way that makes Full metal jacket look like the teletubbies, to make our plentiful and enticing cocktails and our luscious & ridiculously awesome food. Then they bring it.

Come to us. Be our friends. Love us like lost brothers.

(adventurebar.co.uk/about-us)

SMOOCH RINGS

Here's another "about" page I mentioned earlier; apparently it's still the reason why so many customers choose Smooch over its UK competitors. While the page is written in the third person (for various boring reasons), I hope you'll agree that it still comes across as friendly and personable.

THE SMOOCH STORY SO FAR…

After getting a "D" in his Geography O-level — only to receive a "U" after intensive tutoring and a retake – Stephen Slade realised that a career in town planning might not be his best bet. And thank goodness, because his true love is and always has been jewellery.

So at the age of 16, Stephen became an apprentice diamond setter in his dad's jewellery factory. And after many years working in the jewellery industry – first as a diamond setter and then as a salesman – he decided to set up Smooch. He was well aware of the problems couples had with buying wedding rings from jewellery shops (inflexible opening hours, harassed salespeople, overpriced rings and a small variety to choose from), and he thought he had a better solution.

As his wife and kids will tell you, Stephen is rarely right. But 15 years and 50,000 happy couples later, they'll admit he was right about this one.

Smooch continues to go from strength to strength. It started as a one-man-band in 2000, with Stephen driving to visit couples around the country and operating from a child-size desk in the playroom. Six months later, Stephen hired his first two Smooch Advisers and the three of them travelled the country, making couples very happy but the planet a little bit sad: the mileage was pretty insane.

Fast forward 15 years and Smooch now has almost 50 regional Advisers who operate within a roughly 25-mile radius. Stephen's wife Floss (aka The Real Boss) also came on board as co-director.

As well as the Smooch Advisers, there are now 8 much-loved and much-cherished admin employees, who work with Floss and Stephen from Smooch HQ in Harefield. The best bit is that they get to work on proper, adult desks and can use computers rather than crayons.

A few Smooch-wannabes have cropped up over the years – the sincerest form of flattery. But Smooch is still the best:

- *The best coverage around the country (we're certain there'll be an Adviser in your area to visit you)*

- *The best selection of rings*

- *The most flexible options for customis-*

- ing those rings
  - The fairest, most transparent prices
  - The best guarantee – a Lifetime Guarantee – with all rings

If you want to find out more about Smooch, just visit the Contact us page for information on how to reach us.

(smoochrings.co.uk/about-us)

BLU HOMES

An example of non-jokey-yet-awesome text in action:

> *WE LOOKED AT THE HISTORY OF HOME BUILDING AND CAME TO ONE CLEAR CONCLUSION – IT WAS TIME FOR A RADICAL CHANGE*
>
> *Our response was to apply advanced technology to design and build highly personalized, premium prefab homes of extraordinary quality. They had to be beautiful, spacious, and light-filled. We wanted*

to find new ways to bring the outdoors in. Most importantly, our goal was to create homes that people love living in.

A better product

We're constantly perfecting our concept of how to build beautiful homes with spacious lines, soaring ceilings, and walls of glass that seamlessly connect interiors to the outdoors. This design thinking also applies to building better homes for you and the environment.

(This is an excerpt from their "vision" page. See the full page here: bluhomes.com/our-vision)

NUABIKES

Here's a description of one of this bike company's products. You can almost *imagine* the person saying it – and you get a feel for the pride they have in their product, the joy they get from biking, and the geeky obsession they have with every single element of the bike.

Discover the SC-01

We had a clear vision of the perfect urban commuter: a bike that merged form and function, that combined class and performance. One as simple and durable as possible. A machine for those who think that "less but better" is the way to go. €2495

The result of this vision is the single speed SC-01, a high quality, maintenance-free bicycle. Lightweight, stable and responsive, it is a pleasure to ride, and with its elegant and timeless design, it is a pleasure to the eye. It is made to last, with a titanium frame, fork and handlebar, Gates belt transmission, Brooks leather saddle and grips, and other high quality components. The SC-01 will be your urban affairs partner for many decades, without asking anything in return... well, maybe just a little bit of love.

(nuabikes.com)

DOLLAR SHAVE CLUB

Dollar Shave Club (dollarshaveclub.com) has personalityful text in every crevice of its website.

For example, the homepage contains the quote:

"I like shaving with a dull razor" – No one, ever.

Its "gift card" page contains a pre-written message that you can send to the recipient:

I got you a membership in Dollar Shave Club. Yes, it's the greatest gift, probably of all time. Your smiling, smoothly shaved face is all the thanks I need.

And the descriptions of each razor say things like:

A lover's blade.

This is your new razor. And it's also your girlfriend's new razor. Or your boyfriend's. You see, the 4X is also known as the Lover's Blade. It was designed to satisfy the harshest critics of both genders, so you can share your subscription (but not your blades, gross) with someone you care about. It's equally good for the face, legs, armpits, or anything else.

Even the blog is called something fun:

THE BATHROOM MINUTES

Chapter 5
KEEP IT SIMPLE

"Our business is infested with idiots who try to impress by using pretentious jargon."
–David Ogilvy

My husband will occasionally ask me about some grammatical rule or other, and I'll annoy the hell out of him by using phrases like "dangling modifier" and "coordinating conjunction"… at which point he'll roll his eyes and go off to find a *Sesame Street* episode on the topic.

I don't *mean* to make things more complicated than they need to be. Well maybe I do a bit: it's always nice to feel knowledgeable about a topic. But the main problem is that it's hard to unlearn these types of phrases – to explain a concept using ordinary, easy-to-understand words when I've spent so much time using the bigger words.

And herein lies the problem with lots of businesses: **they know too much.** They use industry lingo and discuss complicated issues like the rest of us discuss last night's episode of *Dancing With the Stars*.

When it comes to explaining a tricky concept, being an expert is a weakness: you risk assuming that your reader knows way more than they actually do – and it results in dense, hard-to-understand text that alienates your reader and makes them feel like an idiot.

It's your job to make your reader understand what you'll do for them and why you're so much better than everyone else. They're not going to buy from you unless they know what they're buying – and there's a good chance they'll be grateful that you made it easy to understand (especially when compared to the other providers out there).

So whenever you write something, read it out loud and ask yourself: **will someone outside the industry understand the point I'm making?** Even better, show your writing to a friend and ask them if they understand it.

If the answer is no, rewrite the text – using the simplest words possible. Keep rewriting and rewriting until you end up with something that contains no industry clichés, and no abstract or meaningless phrases (like "integrated solutions" or "dynamic energy" – which are usually there to pad out a sentence and make a business seem more knowledgeable).

There's an exception to this rule: **if you only want to attract people who understand the lingo, use the lingo.** For example, I wrote the website text for a Forex-trading platform based in Australia; its target market is men in their early thirties who like to dabble in currency trading in their spare time because it makes them feel like the powerful, intelligent, manly Wall Street guy they've always wanted to be. The language on this site purposefully uses industry terminology, because it makes the target audience feel like they're part of a knowledgeable inner circle.

> *"As experienced traders ourselves, we built the brokerage service we always wanted. That means*

> *leverage of 500:1, reliable execution and rock-solid infrastructure."*

The text still needs to have personality of course, but it can include words and phrases that only "industry people" would know.

Either way, remember: when you make your reader feel smart, they like you. When they like you, they want to be your customer.

Chapter 6
SELL THE SIZZLE

"People don't want to buy a quarter-inch drill. They want a quarter-inch hole!" –Theodore Levitt

You're an accountant? Great... errr, what's in it for me?

You're a jeweler? Wonderful... so?

You're a business consultant? Interesting... now where's the guy with the crudités?

Almost everyone has heard the phrase "Sell the sizzle, not the steak," yet it's bizarre how few companies actually *do* it. Basically, you need to stop describing WHAT you do. You need to show how your potential customer can BENEFIT from working with you.

People don't *really* want an accountant, or a jeweler, or a business consultant... they want an outcome that these things lead to – such as freedom from worrying about the IRS, or a delighted fiancée, or a way to double their business. You'll be one step closer to getting them as a customer if you can connect the dots and explain the outcome for them. (By the way, saying you do "best practice business consulting" is absolutely *nowhere near* closer to "selling the sizzle." Saying you offer "best practice business consulting" is like saying "this is an edible steak." It means *nothing*.)

So ask yourself: what will people get out of working with you or buying your product?

- The Wow Company (thewowcompany.com) isn't an accountancy firm. It helps small businesses "make more profit, pay less tax, have more fun."

- Tessa Stuart (tessastuart.co.uk) isn't a researcher for food brands. She helps your food products "fly off the shelf."

- Innocent (innocentdrinks.co.uk) isn't a smoothie company. It makes "natural, delicious, healthy drinks that help people live well and die old."

- Zoho (zoho.com) isn't CRM software. It helps you "attract, retain and delight more customers."

The same rule applies to any "features" your service or product offers. If you look at Zoho's "features" website page, you'll see that it doesn't simply list things like "workflow automation," "visitor tracking" and "opportunity-tracking tool." Instead it shares what that means for the customer:

"IMPROVE YOUR WORKFLOW. Write your own rules. Simplify and streamline your sales processes based on your unique business needs. Automatically assign leads and customers to the reps best qualified to handle them."

"VISITOR TRACKING: Intelligently track your visitor's footprint, have a dialog, fascinate with a reliable service, measure and improve the sales conversion rates."

> *"Zoho CRM's Opportunity Tracking tool gives you a current, comprehensive view of all your sales activities. Know where every customer is in the sales cycle, deal size, contact history, even competitor information to help craft more effective messaging. Dynamic Reports & Dashboards provide an easy, accurate read of everything going on."*

And check out Urbanears (urbanears.com) – a company that makes earphones. Unlike so many other earphone companies, Urbanears explains what the features mean *for you*:

> *"Move around freely, pick up calls and listen to music on the go without tangled cords. Hassle-free as it should be! The Plattan ADV Wireless headphone is the first Bluetooth headphone in the Urbanears line-up. It comes with a built in microphone, a swipe interface on the ear cup and it is ready for up to 14-hours solid playtime before recharging."*

By explaining the benefits of both your company and its individual features/services, your future customers will recognize how their needs can be met, and you'll find the entire selling process that much easier.

Also, you'll sound far more exciting at cocktail parties if you say "I help women rinse their cheating ex-husbands for everything they own" instead of "I'm a lawyer."

Chapter 7
GRAB THEIR ATTENTION

"The reader is someone with an attention span of about 30 seconds." –William Zinsser

> *"Your product can be copied in a heartbeat, your prices undercut, your people poached. Uncover the one thing that can never be stolen."*

What's the one thing for *your* business? I don't know: you'll have to ask (well, hire) Beliyf (beliyf.com) – the branding agency responsible for the captivating text above, which is used on its homepage. Whether that kind of scaremongery strategy appeals to you, you have to admit that it's way more grabby and intriguing than:

> *"We are a branding agency based in Old Street, London. From established FTSE 100 companies to ambitious startups, we partner with clients across sectors and industries providing specialist brand consultancy, brand design services and strategic communications expertise."* (Branding agency)

Setting aside the lack of personality, the inability to talk like a human being, the ultimate failure to sell the sizzle, the downright refusal to niche down, and everything else that's wrong with this website introduction, there's one other thing I hate about it: something I call "lazy lack of crafting." Nothing has been done to grab the reader – to intrigue them, make them smile or feel anything for the company.

When you have many competitors and need to set yourself apart from them, "grabbing the reader" is an imperative part of writing for your business. Once you've grabbed them, two things happen:

1. They're likely to keep reading and finding out more about your services/products – which means they're *less likely* to bother reading about other businesses in your in-

dustry.

2. They'll get to know you a bit more – and they'll be more inclined to trust you, like you, and be willing to pay a premium to work with you.

Grab your reader everywhere you write – on the homepage, the "about" page, the "services" page, your promotional emails, your Facebook adverts… everywhere.

It often isn't easy to find an interesting way in – which is why you see so many homepage introductions that have dull, uncreative text that says nothing particularly noteworthy about what sets them apart. Like these:

- *"We focus on innovations, as perfect technologies and global experience make us trendsetters in the construction industry." (Construction company)*

- *"We offer legal advice and aid in solving problems regarding procedures of the law." (Lawyer)*

- *"We're an award winning branding & digital*

agency, passionate about design and always delivering measurable results for our clients." (Branding and digital agency)

- *"Identica is a brand strategy and design agency, where you will find an inspiring team of design, strategy, and production specialists, working together to create, restore and evolve iconic brands." (Brand and design agency)*

Again, let's ignore all the *other* issues with these intros and focus purely on the fact that they're doing nothing to steal the reader's attention and make them think, "Oh, *hello*" when they read the page.

I'm not using decades-old websites as my examples here – the ones belonging to businesses that have since bitten the dust or given up their web presence long ago. I'm using new, stylish, clean and well-designed sites that have won design awards but paid no attention to copywriting. They may look great, but they don't draw the reader in – and I doubt they're all that effective in attracting their dream customers.

Compare the examples above with these companies' homepages:

- *"Trust me, YOU want to see this!" (jakubkaspar.cz – web designer)*

- *"PRINT IS DEAD." (raisethedeadwith.us – printing company)*

- *"ACID TONGUES, SILK DELIVERY. De:strukt are a design studio, tucked up in Glasgow's Hidden Lane. Teaming up with global talent and brands, we create designs with care and clout. We have a wild eye and thumping passion for IDs, street art, still and moving images." (destrukt.co.uk – branding and web design)*

- *"I work with the high achievers of this world – the driven, successful business owners and employees who have no time to take a step back and exhale. I help you to understand yourself and your needs better, feel more energized and be fulfilled in what you do both inside and outside of work." (silkezanker.com – life coach)*

- *"The barbershop used to be more than just a*

> *place to get a haircut or shave; it was a hub of the community where people came together to bond, to socialize and to exchange ideas. With the goal of bringing this camaraderie back in style, Blind Barber… has created a concept that goes well beyond cuts and shaves. By cultivating a men's grooming line, an influential voice, and multiple destinations, Blind Barber has expanded into all realms of the modern man: grooming, cocktails, fashion, and lifestyle." (blindbarber.com – barbershop)*

They've all clearly spent time figuring out what they're about, how they benefit their customers, and what makes them stand apart from the competition. They care less about announcing what they do (as it's usually obvious – especially if you searched for their service on Google or clicked on a link from another site), and instead have thought hard about who they're for. They've then written some text that will appeal directly to their target customer – using an unusual and surprising angle that they know will catch those people's attention.

But like I said before, it's not just the top of the homepage that needs to be attention-grabbing:

potential customers may reach your site via *any* page on your website or *any* of your marketing materials, and you need to grab them there, too. You also want your potential customers to continue to feel excited and thrilled *all the way through* – whichever page they're reading.

Below are a few examples of "ways in" I've written for various businesses:

Classical pianist "about" page:

"Donald, Daffy and my grandmother have a lot to answer for.

They're what inspired me to become a classical composer and pianist. Not Beethoven, nor Mozart – as captivating as they are – but a couple of cartoon characters and a lovely old lady who owned too many aprons."

(See the full page at bit.ly/dancooper.)

Lighting design company "case study" page for Superdry clothes store:

"Retail lighting design in recent years has shifted

from stark, bright interiors that show up every pimple to the complete opposite: dark, moody and club-like stores where you can barely see your own arm.

While Superdry's style is closer to the latter, we overcame the "is this a skirt or a shirt?" problem by illuminating the interior to slightly higher light levels than competitor stores. A club-like and dramatic vibe is still achieved, however, through using narrow-beam spotlights in place of ambient light."

(See the full case study at bit.ly/superdry-lights.)

Real estate agency "about" page:

"It all started with a fax.

It was the summer of 1996, and John Horton knew nothing about real estate. He did know that he owed his mom a lot of money after spending 18 months backpacking around Australia and India. Sick of spending his nights stacking shelves to pay her back, he walked into a local realtor – hoping to use their fax machine to send off an application to a recruitment agency.

It turned into an impromptu job interview, and two days later – still knowing nothing about real estate – John was handed the keys to a company car and sent off to value some houses. Sixteen years later, he's still going – but now at his own company, Horton & Garton, which he opened in 2007 after ten years of working in Hammersmith for a couple of corporate chains."

(See the full page at bit.ly/hgarton.)

Real estate agency "you do the viewings" page:

"They say buyers make up their minds within 30 seconds of entering a property...

...So make those crucial seconds count: let the buyer see your home through the eyes of its biggest fan – you. Even if an estate agent claims to have impeccable local knowledge, they can't beat yours. You know the best places to eat, the prettiest parks, and the as-yet undiscovered cafes... and your enthusiasm will soon have the buyer imagining themselves living in your home."

(See the full page at bit.ly/fishneedwater.)

Becoming a master of attention-grabbing requires creativity, patience, and the modern equivalent of scrunching up notepaper and throwing it angrily at a trash can. But persevere: the effort will pay off.

QUICK TIPS FOR GETTING GRABBY

Try applying these tips to something you've already written. Or if you're feeling super keen, you could pick a random "about" page online and attempt to write a grabbier version.

- **Learn from the best!** Pay attention to other people's writing that grabs you. It doesn't just have to be websites or marketing copy – it can be newspaper and magazine articles, blog posts, product packaging, even adverts (including those on Facebook). You'll find yourself learning from it without even realizing. When it comes to articles (either print or online), find some writers you admire, read all their stuff, and pay particularly close attention to the opening paragraph.

- **Wikipedia is your friend.** Use it to find out more about your industry, your local area (which could come in useful for the "about" page), your competitors, your clients… everything. It's often surprising what you can learn – and how it can then be used as an interesting angle in your copy.

For example, I recently wrote some case studies for the website of a lighting design company. One of their projects was "Escalator 3" at Harrods in London. Here are the first couple of paragraphs of my case study:

"Back in 1898, Harrods debuted England's first ever escalator: a woven leather unit that operated like a conveyor belt, where nervous customers were offered brandy at the top to help them recover from their ordeal.

Escalators have come on a long way since then – in particular Escalator 3 at the very same Knightsbridge store. It's the centrepiece of an extensive retrofit that includes 16 new escalators over eight floors…"

That introduction is down to Wikipedia: I didn't know it before doing my research, and the client didn't either.

Be sure to fact-check any information you're thinking of using by going to the list of sources at the bottom of the page.

- **Avoid using hackneyed introductions** that lost all semblance of humor or cleverness years ago. These include "It is a truth universally acknowledged…" and "Webster's Dictionary defines [something] as…"

- **When you niche down, being grabby gets miles easier.** All you need to do is write "Dog training in Seattle for labradoodles" or "Accountancy for physiotherapists in Nevada" or "High fashion for 6-foot women" and the right customer will sit up and take notice. That doesn't mean you can get lazy though: you may have the skills they require, but people still need to like how you come across and approve of what you stand for. That's why I love this "about" page text from Fat Yoga in Portland, Oregon – it niches down *and* has a clear, confident personality:

"The Thing About Fat Yoga

First and most obvious, Fat Yoga classes are tailored to people who may not be the stereotypical yoga student. While most of us identify as fat, it's certainly not a requirement for participation. You do NOT need to be a specific size to be welcome at Fat Yoga.

Poses are presented and modified to each individual's ability. The size of our thighs, arms, bellies, and butts all change the way we are capable of expressing the traditional asanas (poses). Fat Yoga honors and embraces our differences and strives to create an environment where all bodies can do all poses.

Fat Yoga has no objective or claim towards weight loss. Frankly, we are not interested in it. We focus on strength building, flexibility, balance, self-acceptance and peace of mind. There is

> *much evidence of yoga's transformative powers. Through a committed yoga practice, we can embrace our relationship with our bodies and find joy in movement."* (fatyoga.org/About.html)

Remember: it's surprisingly tricky to create attention-grabbing text, so please try not to be put off if you don't manage it first time. If you want more help (in the form of activities, worksheets, advice and tips), be sure to sign up to my Business Writing Bootcamp: there's an entire lesson dedicated to the topic. Visit **yourattentionplease.co/bootcamp** to get started.

Chapter 8
FOLLOW YOUR OWN PATH

"In a busy marketplace, not standing out is the same as being invisible." –Seth Godin

Let's be honest: if your competitor jumped off a cliff, it'd be good for business, right? "Delighted" might be too strong a word, but just think about all those new customers you could nab! What you most certainly *wouldn't* do is jump straight off that cliff after them.

So why are you copying what your competitor is up to right now?

I have a lot of bugbears when it comes to business writing ("NO! Really?!"), but "competitor copying" is one of my biggest. My disapproval isn't for moral reasons or because I think you should do your own damn work; the reason I get frustrated is because you're inadvertently making life harder for yourself.

When you copy what's on your competitor's homepage, or the words they use on their "about" page, or the offers in their Facebook ads, or the information in their brochures, yes: it indicates a massive lack of confidence and independent thought on your part. But it also contributes to the vicious cycle of crap writing that permeates all industries.

Bear this in mind: that competitor you're copying has no doubt copied *another* business in the industry. And because most companies don't know what they're doing when it comes to writing, it's likely you're all going very badly wrong without realizing it. You're ALL making life harder for yourselves when it comes to attracting the right customers who'd be delighted to work with you.

This "copying epidemic" is to blame for all businesses saying the same things and offering their potential customers no real point of difference. It's likely that the text involves absolutely no personality or sizzle – and that it doesn't "niche down" to appeal to just one type of company. Even if it *does* do those things, you'll all have the *same* personality, offer the *same* sizzle, and be attempting to niche down to the exact *same* people.

It's a lose-lose.

You need to be different. Don't look to what the others in your industry are doing: figure out for yourself what you stand for, why you're different, and what sort of customer you want to appeal to. *Then* write, and don't look sideways.

Chapter 9
SHOW, DON'T TELL

"Don't tell me the moon is shining; show me the glint of light on broken glass." –Anton Chekhov

There's one particularly heinous crime that your competitors are probably committing, and it's something you need to take care to avoid: they *tell* us they're great, without making any effort to show why we should believe them.

They offer "innovative solutions," a "world-class service," "excellent customer service," a "collaborative process," and many other abstract phrases. They're also obsessed with saying how "passionate" they are – usually about "your success," "your happiness," "your business," or "customer service." And for everything they do, they "strive" for it, "pride" themselves in it, "have you covered," and can be "counted on" to "exceed expectations."

These words are meaningless by themselves, and they fool no one. Seriously: no reader is going to think to themselves, "Oh wow: this plumber says he's passionate about customer service. Decision made!"

Rather than announce what you consider your selling points to be, *show* them by describing what you do (with excitement and energy), and let readers decide for themselves.

Here are some companies that have nailed the concept of "show, don't tell":

- Barbara Fernandez (aka Rocking Raw Chef: rockingrawchef.com) is clearly "passionate" about helping busy moms prepare quick, healthy and delicious raw food meals. But she doesn't use the word "passionate" once. Even her "contact" page is brimming with enthusiasm:

> *"Say hello!*
> *I mean it! I ADORE what I do – and talking about it! – so let me know if you have a quick question."*

- Sofas & Stuff (sofasandstuff.com) don't just say they have "high-quality products" or that they provide "excellent customer service": they do a fantastic job of *showing* it instead. There's an example of their text coming up.

- Web developers Infinum have a page on their site called "Our stuff" (infinum.co/our-stuff), which showcases the projects they work on in their spare time – when not doing client work. Without saying a word, they show just how passionate they are about their work: they're even willing to do it when not getting paid.

Next up: some longer extracts from other companies, to help you see just how effective it can be.

MASTERS OF "SHOW, DON'T TELL"

SOFAS AND STUFF

Made in Britain.

We make all of our sofas and beds in England. We're pretty proud of this.

Unlike most things nowadays, that seem to be made in the Far East or Eastern Europe, the UK is still a powerhouse in making really beautiful, great quality sofas, using traditional skills honed over hundreds of years.

Lifetime construction guarantee.

All our sofas carry a lifetime construction guarantee. It covers the feet and frame, springs, webbing, and sofabed mechanisms. Everything you can't see, except the seat cushion fillings. But don't worry about them. They'll retain their shape and comfort for years. Why? Read on.

The cushion.

Our in-house expert (my wife, Julia) has found that when someone's unhappy with a sofa, the seat cushions are mostly to blame.

There isn't much new technology in our sofas; we like to make them the traditional way. Our cushions however are a veritable hotbed of innovation, and our Quallofil Supreme interiors are, according to FIRA, (the Furniture Industry Research Association) the best on the market, for returning to their original shape, after plumping. This is because we use new Monopolymer fibre; pause for large yawn. To you and I this means the fibres act like a coiled spring. Need I say any more? Yes I do, on second thoughts. Even coiled springs if they are never turned will loose their elasticity. So the key to good maintenance of your fibre seat cushions is to turn them regularly and give them a good regular pummelling. I cannot stress this point enough.

(This is an excerpt. See the full page by visiting sofasandstuff.com and clicking on the page called "Beneath the covers.")

DISHOOM (RESTAURANT)

Some excerpts from the drinks menu:

EDWINA'S AFFAIR: The hush-hush love triangle of gin, rose and cardamom, in a secret garden of fresh mint, strewn with candied rose petals. Light, refreshing, captivating.

1948 SOUR: Dry whisky tannins play with the creamy foam of egg-white. Peach, hibiscus, honey, fresh lemon and India's highly acclaimed whisky Amrut — nectar of the gods from the churning ocean.

THE COMMANDER: Serious and strong with a dash of scandal, much like the upstanding Commander Nanavati, who shot his English wife's lover with a navy pistol then handed himself in. A bone-dry martini of pepper-washed Royal Dock Navy Strength gin, Kamm & Sons liqueur and a naughty absinthe rinse.

IPA PAANCH: Convince yourself of masculinity: tastes of tobacco, leather and peat are here in Dishoom hop-infused gin, lime, jaggery, English

Breakfast Tea and spices. Your expression will be serious.

VICEROY'S OLD-FASHIONED: *The sort of drink in which Lord Mountbatten may have found welcome repose. A bottleaged muddle of Woodford Reserve bourbon, bayleaf reduction, green tea and so on. Like an old Raj club-room, with tertiary colours and artistic composition.*

(dishoom.com)

THE GINGER PIG (BUTCHER)

From the "Sausages" page on their website:

Sausage making is an important part of nose to tail butchery; in getting the most from an animal and ensuring nothing valuable is wasted. In the days before refrigeration – when the whole pig needed to be cooked or set to cure in a day or so – sausages would be quite strongly flavoured with plenty of herbs and seasoning, and either eaten that day or hung above the fire to dry so that they would keep a while. As refrigeration became possible we moved towards a fresher sausage, with just a little salt and flavouring, intended for eating within a couple of days.

We've been making sausages since The Ginger Pig first began, and although we must have made hundreds of varieties since then, the core range described below are still our most popular. We might have five or six additional varieties on display in the counter, depending on what the butchers in our shops are making that week – including recipes such as classic Italian, venison and juniper, pork and apple or beef and chilli.

We use a blend of pork belly and shoulder to ensure a good fat content, which bastes the sausages from the inside as they cook. With the exception of our Old Spot and Toulouse/Garlic Toulouse sausages, which are pure meat and intended for stewing, we use around 20% breadcrumbs in the mix. This helps to retain succulence as they cook – the 'juice' stays in the sausage rather than escaping into the pan.

(thegingerpig.co.uk)

Chapter 10
STAY LEAN

"I didn't have time to write a short letter, so I wrote a long one instead." –Mark Twain

A few years ago, my husband and I decided to become "digital nomads" – people who travel while they work – because all we need to run our businesses are a couple of laptops and half-decent wifi connection.

When we started traveling, we had two humongous wheeled suitcases weighing a total of 50kg. Over time we whittled and whittled down – replacing our piles of clothes for a few lightweight, harder-wearing technical items that are good for all seasons – and today we travel the world with just two small backpacks weighing 8.5kg each.

Why, exactly, am I telling you about the history of my clothing? Because you can achieve something similar with your text: you can make it leaner and more hardworking. You can remove lots of flabby, unnecessary words and replace them with a few stronger, more effective ones (just like my lightweight insulated jacket and my ultra-thin merino wool socks).

"Lean text" doesn't mean "loss of personality" – so don't try that one on me. In fact, quite the opposite is true: when you use lots of words to make a point, your personality goes missing under all the verbiage, your point becomes harder to understand, and you waste your reader's valuable time.

You'll be surprised by just how much flab you can cut. For example, you can get from this (from a real-life website):

> *"In order to get the most from your pool heater, whatever system type or brand it is, it needs to be routinely taken care of. There may come a time when your pool heater is no longer functioning properly. Perhaps it cannot handle your temperature requirements on a chilly evening, or it fails to*

start up at your beck and call. We offer excellent pool heater repair service in Las Vegas, NV 24/7, so you won't have to wait long for your warm swimming pool to be restored." (Plumbing company)

To this:

"Is your pool heater misbehaving? If it isn't heating up quickly enough (or at all), we're available 24/7 to come over and repair it."

Without breaking a sweat.

Actually, scratch that: I *say* "without breaking a sweat," but admittedly it's much harder to cull your own writing than other people's. If you find yourself sobbing "YOU DON'T DESERVE THIS, LITTLE WORD," take a moment, say your goodbyes, and follow these tips:

1: Go back to Chapter 3 on "being a human," and follow the advice there.

2: Get rid of your first paragraph. It's bound to be some sort of unnecessary scene-setting for the real stuff that's coming next.

3: Figure out what your main point is, write that, and remove everything else around it.

4: It's very likely you can remove the word "very" from your sentences.

5: You'll really benefit from removing "really" as well.

Chapter 11
CRUSH BAD GRAMMAR

"If it's not extra-marital sex… it is perhaps extra marital sex, which is quite a different bunch of coconuts." –Lynne Truss

You *need* to care about grammar. Why? Because – rightly or wrongly – people will make judgements about your business based on the quality of your writing.

Bad writing makes you look unprofessional, and it gives the impression that you don't pay attention to detail. (People might not be able to detect *what* is wrong with the text – they'll just know it isn't right in some way.) Most importantly though, bad writing is also much more difficult to read and understand – and it immediately makes life harder for your potential customers. It only takes one confusing sentence for a reader to give up and wander off.

The good news for you is that bad business writing is EVERYWHERE – scattered across websites, sales pages and promotional emails far and wide. By fixing your own text, you'll immediately be doing better than most of your competitors.

Now… I can (and will, if given half the chance) talk for days about grammar. I have a feeling you won't appreciate knowing absolutely everything I have to say on the topic though, so I've decided to simply whip through the four most rampant grammatical mistakes I see in business writing – which are also the ones that will make the biggest difference to how you come across.

I promise this'll be quick…

MISTAKE #1: WILLY-NILLY HYPHENS

Hyphens aren't artistic flourishes: you don't just add one every now and again to make the page prettier. While they're misused in a number of ways by writers, I'm going to focus on the one most consistent mistake I see – and here's a sentence to remember it by:

"If you want to save time, follow this time-saving tip."

Here goes…

When you have a phrase where two or more words are describing one object or concept, you'll need a hyphen in there somewhere. (Those "describing words" are known as "compound adjectives.")

For example:

- "Three-year deal"
- "Old-fashioned restaurant"
- "Long-term contract"

If you were to remove the hyphen in the phrases above, they'd look confusing.

If, however, you switch the sentence around so that the object comes *first,* you don't need the hyphen:

- "The deal is for three years."
- "The restaurant is old fashioned."
- "The contract is long term."

BUT (of course there's a "but")…

If the compound adjective contains an adverb ending in -ly (quickly, badly, etc.), the -ly suffix is enough to alert the readers to the meaning of the phrase, and a hyphen isn't needed. (An adverb is simply a word that tweaks the meaning of another word – so "Our dog sleeps peacefully on the floor" <– "peacefully" is the adverb.)

So:

- "We're highly respected in our industry."
- "We're known for our beautifully crafted furnishings."
- "We'll return your newly cleaned labradoodle to you in the morning."

Occasionally, the lack or addition of a hyphen can cause the phrase to change meaning completely, so it's important to get it right. E.g.

- "Take advantage of our new customer discount." / "Take advantage of our new-customer discount."

- "We're selling a little used car." / "We're selling a little-used car."

- "She never gives tips to black cab drivers." / "She never gives tips to black-cab drivers."

To be honest, this isn't even the half of it when it comes to hyphen rules – but it should be more than enough to help you avoid the commonest, peskiest of mistakes.

MISTAKE #2: COMMA SPLICES

Comma splices make copy editors angrier than almost anything else in life.

Here's what you need to know:

A comma splice is the attempt to join two independent clauses (two parts of a sentence that could easily be a sentence in their own right) with nothing but a comma.

Example:

"We plan to grow our business by 50% over the next two years, after that we'll consolidate and concentrate on profitability."

Both parts of that sentence could be sentences on their own ("We plan to grow our business by 50% over the next two years" and "After that we'll consolidate and concentrate on profitability"). When you bash them together and shove a comma in between, that's a comma splice. It's lazy writing, basically: the writer can't figure out how to connect the two clauses, so just inserts a comma there and goes off to make a cup of coffee.

Here are a couple more examples of sentences with comma splices:

"Thank you for the guidance, it is very helpful."

"Sign up today, the conference will fill quickly."

How do you fix a comma splice? You have two main options:

1: Find a better way to join the two independent clauses

You could use the semi-colon: "We plan to grow our business by 50% over the next two years; after that we'll consolidate and concentrate on profitability."

Or maybe you'd prefer a dash: "We plan to grow our business by 50% over the next two years – after that we'll consolidate and concentrate on profitability."

Or perhaps you'd like a "connecting word" to go after the comma, like "and": "We plan to grow our business by 50% over the next two years, and after that we'll consolidate and concentrate on profitability."

2: Separate the two independent clauses

"We plan to grow our business by 50% over the next two years. After that we'll consolidate and concentrate on profitability."

The thing to bear in mind is that commas are good at holding *small* things together – like single words.

Independent clauses are bigger and more important, and they require more than a comma to hold them together. Think of a comma as bad-quality duct tape.

MISTAKE #3: RUN-ON SENTENCES

A run-on sentence is two independent clauses joined together without *any* form of punctuation.

"We plan to grow our business by 50% over the next two years after that we'll consolidate and concentrate on profitability."

"We read your application we thought it was excellent."

You can fix a run-on sentence in the same way that you'd fix a comma splice.

MISTAKE #4: MIXING UP WORDS

Here are some of the most common culprits:

They're / there / their

- "They're" is a contraction of "they are": "They're more than happy to help you." (Try replacing "they're" with "they are"; if it still makes sense, you know that "they're" is correct.)

- "There" is the opposite of "here": "We've just opened a new store over there."

- "Their" shows possession – that something belongs to them: "Their office is gigantic."

You're / your

- "You're" is a contraction of "you are": "You're such a great customer." (Try replacing "you're" with "you are"; if it still makes sense, you know that "you're" is correct.)

- "Your" shows possession – that something belongs to you: "Your comfort is very important to us."

It's / its

- "It's" is usually a contraction of "it is": "It's going to be a great day." Sometimes, it's a contraction of "it has": "It's been a long day." (Try replacing "it's" with "it is" and "it has"; if it still makes sense, you know "it's" is correct.)

- "Its" shows possession – that something belongs to it: "The rest of its funding comes from private investment."

Everyday / every day

- "Everyday" means ordinary/common: "These shoes are great for everyday wear."

- "Every day" means "each day": "We're open every day."

If you're not sure which one to use, try replacing "everyday"/"every day" with "each day". If "each day" makes sense in the context of the sentence, then you want the two-word form: "every day."

Compliment / complement

- "Compliment" with an "i" is a kind or flattering remark: "They complimented us on our fresh ideas and vision."

- "Complement" with an "e" refers to something that completes or goes well with something: "The new service complements our existing facilities."

Remember it like this: "**I** like to give compl**i**ments"; "Complements complete things."

Affect / effect

- "Affect" usually means "to influence": it *does* something to something or someone else. "The rain affected our journey time." / "The change will affect your retirement fund."

- "Effect" has a lot of subtle meanings, but the main one is that it indicates a "result" of some kind: "The effect was astonishing." / "The medicine had no effect on her condition."

If you struggle to figure out which is which, try the "good or bad" trick: if you can insert "good" or "bad" in front of the word (and the sentence still makes sense), the correct choice will almost always be "effect."

- "The medicine had no [good] effect on her

condition." <– Still makes sense.

- "The change will [bad] affect your retirement fund." <– Makes no sense.

***

As I said before, the world isn't lacking in bad grammar. If you follow the rules in this chapter and the other guidance throughout this book, you'll be free from the most annoying and destructive mistakes. You don't need to be perfect – just good enough to avoid putting off your reader.

Chapter 12
BLAST THROUGH WRITER'S BLOCK

"The first draft of anything is shit."
–Ernest Hemingway

Lessons over: it's time to put everything into practice and get writing!

But... oh, wait... the dreaded blankness...

Getting started with a blank sheet of screen is daunting to say the least, so here's what I suggest you do first:

Create an avatar.

An avatar is a fictitious person created by you, who

embodies your ideal customer.

When you create an avatar, your intention is to go deep into that person's life, their interests, their fears, their desires, the words they use and the phrases they simply don't understand. It's about far more than "niching down" to a particular section of the market (which I talked about in Chapter 2).

By having an avatar in mind when you write, you'll find it much easier to follow all the guidance in this book:

- You'll be thinking about a particular person when you write, so you'll prevent yourself from wandering off into a cliché-filled land of corporate nonsense – because your avatar wouldn't be able to understand it or would find it off-putting.

- Your avatar will appreciate and admire your personality, so you'll keep that up in all aspects of your writing.

- If your avatar doesn't know any tricky terminology associated with your business, you'll automatically "keep it simple" and use words and phrases they're bound to understand.

- With an avatar in mind, you're more likely to think in terms of how a particular feature or service will actually benefit them – rather than just write down *what* the feature or service is.

- You'll know what will grab your reader and retain their interest, so "finding the right angle" will become more intuitive.

How to create an avatar for your business:

Imagine you're introducing your avatar to a good friend, in a LOT of detail! One of my clients created her avatar before I'd even started working with her. Not only did she describe this avatar (Miranda) in extensive detail, but she also created a separate document of "a day in the life" of the avatar. It may seem silly, but it makes decision-making so much more enjoyable and intuitive along the way.

Your avatar *is* fictional, but it should be based on

reality. Think about customer conversations you've had, or people you've spoken to when doing market research. Their language, story, needs and priorities will help you come up with an even richer, more detailed avatar.

For some of my clients, I've helped them create two avatars – a primary one and a secondary one. The primary avatar is the *main* target customer, and they're at the forefront of my mind when writing their text; the secondary avatar is an altogether different kind of person who might also be interested in the company's services – and I bear them in mind when writing.

Here are some things to think about when creating your avatar:

1: Your avatar's demographic

- Is this person male or female?

- (Imagining he's male…) Where does he live?

- What's his name?

- What does he look like? (Height, weight, hair, clothing, shoes, etc.)

- How old is he?

- What does he do for a living?

- What does a typical day look like for him?

- What does he do for fun?

- What are his political views?

- Where does he go on vacation?

- What kind of personality does he have? (Fiery, friendly, uptight, panicky, reserved, impatient, shy, etc.)

If your business is B2B, have in mind the person who makes the buying decision at the other company. You might want to ask extra questions like:

- What is her job title and role?

- What is she responsible for doing at the company?

- Who does she report to?

2: Your avatar's needs/priorities

If you're serving general consumers (B2C), you can ask questions like these:

- What's his biggest desire? (E.g. you're a nutritionist, and his biggest desire is to lose weight healthily.)

- What's his biggest problem? (E.g. he has a family of five to feed and a very busy job – there's little time for healthy meals.)

- How can you help him right now? (E.g. could you give him a free meal plan for a week, which will help him realize that you really know your stuff and can help more in the future?)

  This can help you figure out what sorts of services to offer – or how to describe your products – on your website or marketing materials. It'll also make sure you don't succumb to the lazy tactic of "Sign up for our free newsletter!!!" – which is an enticing offer to practically no one. (If you want to get people on a mailing list, give them something they really want in return. Here's a great blog post on how to get people on your list: copyblogger.com/betty-crocker-email-marketing.)

If you're serving other businesses (B2B), these questions might also come in useful:

- What does "success" mean to her, in the context of her job?

- What are her biggest challenges to doing a good job?

3: Where to find your avatar

- What websites/blogs does he read? (Their style and tone may help to influence your own.)

- What forums does he visit?

- What pages does he "like" on Facebook?

- What's he Googling for information on?

- Does he listen to podcasts/watch YouTube videos? (If so, what?)

- What events does he attend?

- Is he the type of person who'd be happy to receive a regular email from you, or will he unsubscribe the nanosecond he realizes you contact him more than once a month?

All of the above might seem like a lot of effort, but it works: it helps to create an impression of a fully fledged, real-life human being in your mind, which in turn gives you more of an instinctive feel for how to write to them.

CONCLUSION

You're ready! You now know how to write in a way that captivates and convinces your dream customers – the ones you'll love working with. Those customers meanwhile, will be just as excited about working with or buying from you: your text addresses their exact needs, and it does so in a way that's easy to read and full of personality.

A warning though: from now on you'll spend far more time agonizing over words and phrases than you ever thought possible – and I'm afraid it might not get much easier or quicker, even with practice. I've been known to take up to 90 minutes to write a single paragraph for a client, but you know what? That paragraph was damn good. Yours will be too, and the payoff will be worth it.

Practice is *essential* though. I could have made this book twice as long with more examples and explanations, but I decided against it. Why? Because I believe this book *already* gives you enough of the theory; you won't improve unless you take the time to apply what you've learned to real-life text.

That's why I created my **FREE Business Writing Bootcamp for you: yourattentionplease.co/bootcamp.** It's a six-part email series that contains activities, exercises, templates and worksheets galore – and it'll help you get started on writing your own captivating, enticing and profit-generating text. The course also includes guidance on how to pinpoint what you stand for, how to make your words more attention-grabbing, how to make use of your new avatar, and much more. Sign up today to get started.

Enjoy playing around with your new writing skills, and get ready to relish being the least boring business around!

THANK YOUS

Shayna Oliveira, Christopher Sutton, Pete Domican, Louise Rees, Lewis Smith, Kelly O'Laughlin, Michael Anderson, Andrew Skatteb, Anouk Janssens-Bevernage, Lydia C, Louise Caridia, Mirjana Pogacic, Rohit Gandrakota, Julian Barton, Kara Byun, Lindsey Nubern, Matthias Sommeregger, Cecil Rozeron, Tricia Krohn and David Nix: THANK YOU for being the very first eyes on my project – for detecting all the typos and noticing when sentences could be tightened or lame jokes removed. Your tremendous advice and recommendations have improved this book *at least* three-hundred-fold, and I'm so grateful for all your help.

Andy Scott, Nick Jones, Mark Gilbert, Meredith Williams, Annie Cheney, Ruth Vahle, Casey Stevens, Jacquelyn Dwyer, Steve Sculley, Wilfredo Cocco, Erica Murdoch, Sarah Riley, Kirsten D, Sue Sames, Henry Macintosh, Cindy Hervig, Cristina

Capaz, Floss Slade (aka "mum"), Lori Williams and Josh Adams: you're delightful. Thank you for being so generous with your time and suggestions, and for putting up with all my super-lame quandaries and concerns.

Special shout-out to Tish Daniel for coming up with the name for this book!

Robbie D: you're still the absolute best person ever. EVER.

ABOUT THE AUTHOR

Mish Slade is the founder of a copywriting agency called Mortified Cow, which tells you everything you need to know about her tolerance for stuffy, buttoned-up business writing. She's likely to throw her laptop through a window if she reads one more mention of "delivering measurable results," and figured writing this book would be cheaper than buying a replacement.

You can contact her at mortifiedcow.com

Printed in Great Britain
by Amazon